Here's what people are saying about
THE REVLON SLOUGH

"*The Revlon Slough* is the rare evidence of a life well listened to. Moments are whittled to their barest elements, elements become magnets drawn to synergy, and precisely distilled vignettes are the result. Those following DiZazzo's career will see his versatility coalesce; new readers will discover poetic gold as they dig through the snapshots."

—Cameron Conaway, author of
Malaria, Poems, an NPR Best Book of 2014

"Ray DiZazzo's imaginative new and selected poems, The Revlon Slough, has managed to do the nearly impossible: to enter into the minds and experiences of the human and non-human world he imagines with both fresh imagery and insight. His poems about animals—from a humble mouse to a black widow spider munching on an unsuspecting mate—prove him to be a worthy successor to the work of Galway Kinnell. It is all a matter of perspective, the ability to get out of one's own way in this complex and alienating world, and find a common humanity, a shared wisdom. A life observed with a keen and surprising vision."

—Laurel Ann Bogen
Poet, writer, literary curator, author of
*Psychosis in the Produce Department:
New and Selected Poems 1975-2015* (2016)

"Ray DiZazzo is a wordsmith whose poetry is inspired from a life-long journey of human experience. *The Revlon Slough* lays those experiences bare for his readers with a wide range of poems: strident, and moving, heartfelt and nostalgic, some loving and some cruel and irreverent. DiZazzo's poems exist entirely to serve the reader: they are easily read and understood and they connect and take hold with the grip of powerful imagery."

—Ralph Philips
Writer, scriptwriter, producer and director

'In *The Revlon Slough*, Ray DiZazzo's poetry reflects the influence of poets like James Dickey, Margaret Atwood and Robert Peters. Incorporating his unusual perceptions and vivid craftsmanship to bring them to life in the readers' mind's eye. His view of life and its many complexities is refreshing, sometimes inspiring, sometimes self-incriminating and often simply our unspoken truths, words we have often thought but never put down on paper, told through striking imagery. His is a book well worth reading."

—Ned Rodgers
Corporate media writer, producer, director

"What Ray DiZazzo has written is a series of vivid, emotional experiences coming from the printed page into the readers' hearts and souls....He has managed to powerfully communicate the intimate thoughts and feelings that many, if not all of us, experience, but never find ways to express."

—Phillips Wylly
Writer, producer, director

THE
REVLON
SLOUGH

THE
REVLON
SLOUGH

NEW AND SELECTED POEMS

RAY DIZAZZO

Introduction by Claire Millikin

NEW YORK

www.2leafpress.org

P.O. Box 4378
Grand Central Station
New York, New York 10163-4378
editor@2leafpress.org
www.2leafpress.org

2LEAF PRESS
is an imprint of the
Intercultural Alliance of Artists & Scholars, Inc. (IAAS),
a NY-based nonprofit 501(c)(3) organization that promotes
multicultural literature and literacy.
www.theiaas.org

Copyright © 2018 Ray DiZazzo

Book layout and design: Gabrielle David
Poetry editor: Sean Dillon

Library of Congress Control Number: 2017963110

ISBN-13: 978-1-940939-69-8 (Paperback)
ISBN-13: 978-1-940939-82-7 (eBook)

10   9   8   7   6   5   4   3   2   1

Published in the United States of America

First Edition | First Printing

2LEAF PRESS trade distribution is handled by University of Chicago Press / Chicago Distribution Center (www.press.uchicago.edu) 773.702.7010. Titles are also available for corporate, premium, and special sales. Please direct inquiries to the UCP Sales Department, 773.702.7248.

For Patti, Sunday, Sean and Robert Peters.

CONTENTS

DAMAGED 🐗 33

GALLERY ← 59

COMING ATTRACTIONS ➤ 105

DREAMRUBBLE ~ 113

ANGELS ~ 123

EPILOGUE ~ 131

REVLON AND **SLOUGH?**

I'VE BEEN ASKED how I came up with *The Revlon Slough* as a title for a book of poems. There's an interesting story behind it.

On a Sunday afternoon drive through the farmlands of Camarillo, California, a road-side sign briefly caught my eye. Something about it seemed odd, I made a U-turn and drove back for a second look. Sure enough, on that official city notification sign scrawled with graffiti and stained with mud, I saw what I thought at the time was a disturbingly unlikely combination of words:

"The Revlon Slough"

"Revlon" and "Slough?" Two words I would never have expected to see side-by-side. A juxtaposition of beauty and ugliness; perfume and stench; lipstick and mud. Who in the world would name a slough "Revlon"?

I went on with my drive that day, but I couldn't get those two words out of my mind. It took a few weeks of thinking and scratching out notes, not only about the poem I'd begun to write, but also why the sign had struck me so intensely. After all, they were only a few words that named an obscure, muddy rut winding through several miles of Southern California farmland.

Eventually, I realized that my fascination with those two words and my motivation to expand them into a poem was not because they juxtaposed *opposite* ideas, but for two different reasons. First, because I am a "word person." Words matter to me—how they are written, placed together on a page (albeit in this case a sign) viewed, heard and interpreted by a reader. And in this case, these two words just didn't seem right when placed together. Second, because rather than representing two separate ideas—beauty and ugliness—I realized the words could just as easily represent a single idea viewed from two opposing *perspectives:* Mud and silt may be considered ugly by some, but to others they are just as beautiful as pouty red lips and lovely lashes. Thus:

> Beauty cannot be defined by one set of eyes or one opinion. Beauty encompasses literally everything, and "everything" includes what some consider ugly.

So I had my answer. And after giving it more thought I realized that, depending on the readers' perspective, many of the poems in this collection can suggest both ugliness and beauty, which made it a perfect title for the book as well.

That should have been the end of the story, but I drove past that same sign a few weeks later and got a surprise. When I'd first seen it, the words had been partially obscured with graffiti and mud streaks. As it turns out, the name was not "Revlon" but instead, "Revolon!" I had missed the initial "o" and spent weeks working on a poem and book title based on a mistaken identity!

That prompted a series of Internet searches, phone calls and emails, which eventually led me to the Camarillo Library and a talented young researcher who discovered the origin of the name.

"The Revolon Slough" had been named after a French woman and her two sons who many years earlier had lived in and farmed the area.

But this raised yet another question: was my original premise for the poem still valid? Was the title of the book? After giving it more thought, I decided that the essence of this work had sprung from a unique and revealing experience, and it certainly fit the definition of beauty and ugliness, so I would leave the title (with this note of correction) as I had first seen it.

Though some of these poems were written in my early years and published in various venues, many are recent and unpublished prior to this volume. Some are dark and abrasive, while others are more subtle and at times humorous. Some are morally *safe* and others push the boundaries of what many will consider acceptable. I have no explanation, justification, or reason for any of this work, except to say that when it comes to poetry, I have little desire to write about myself when there are so many other more interesting and relevant subjects, but whatever the ideas my primary aim has always been to explore the art of creating vivid imagery with words—writing that allows readers to experience ideas, instead of simply reading them on the page or hearing them read aloud.

I have divided this book into seven sections. "Marvelous Creatures" is a celebration of animals, birds, and other living things that have always fascinated me. I felt their *stories* should be told first because their place in nature and on my list of ideas to explore, ranks very high. "Damaged" explores the personalities and experiences of the hurt and broken among us and the worlds they (and we) inhabit. "Gallery" is a series of poems that describe individuals, places, and happenings that surround us and continually move in and out of our lives. In "Coming Attractions," I have included four futuristic poems from my first book, *Clovin's Head,* written forty years ago. Though they represent some of my earliest work, I feel they still remain worthy. "Dream Rubble" recounts a number of bizarre, fragmented dream experiences. And for reasons I cannot explain, in the "Angels" section I have begun trying to reshape the image of angels, into something like tiny, ethereal songbirds or mysterious, magical little pups. Go figure! And finally "Epilogue" a single poem, perhaps to sentimental, dedicated to the woman who has loved and supported me for so many years.

With that, let me close by saying that although I hope you find these poems are engaging, provocative and meaningful, my concern is not so much whether you approve of, understand, or even like them. I am fulfilled if you simply experience them.

—Ray DiZazzo
February, 2018

THE BROKEN LINE

RAY DIZAZZO KNOWS the broken line—the starkest poetic tool. It's an honest business, making a life's work through song honed by fracture. Wry and sharp and true, his language cuts, exposing the force of what's real, the intimacy of what holds us listening. The poems of *The Revlon Slough* speak and are a lifetime. New and selected, as the subtitle says, they span decades (his first book appeared in 1976), and while their tone and topics are as various and conflicted as the American experience itself—the timeframe of his poems reaches from Nixon to Trump—the poems riff off the power of language to transform and transcend a markedly imperfect world. They use language as a way to gather the fallen pieces.

Take these words from "The Stew Cutter":

> "Only thing I know," he says
> "besides a cleaver and a lean stew
> is how to play guitar." (p. 46)

The stew cutter manages his tool, and his music, with only a few fingers left on his hands ("whitish nubs and a muscled thumb"). Irony and gallows humor make the poetics of pathos so striking in these lines (it could be the blues—almost a refrain). The stew cutter plays things as they are. And that's DiZazzo's way in this collection — the beauty of neither inflection nor innuendo, but more a syncopated and precise poetics of accident and composure, as American as jazz.

The Revlon Slough (the title itself is based on a misprision — "Revolon Slough" is a California landscape feature) opens with a trickily engaging bestiary. However, these animal poems are no petting zoo, they often bite. Even so, one also finds pools of lyric stillness in the fine observation of poems like "Toad Night Haiku":

> An avocado
> sized southern bull, swelling in
> the hum of insects (p. 25)

Rather more starkly, the birds and beasts and bugs in DiZazzo's "Marvelous Creatures" section play the same tune as his stew cutter. In the first poem of the book, the poet learns from a hunting red tail hawk how "to / a perfect / down-line," ending in a cleaver-quick act of "evisceration" ("To a Red Tail," p. 9). This "perfect down-line" is an apt metaphor for DiZazzo's muse and gift.

To me, the heart of *The Revlon Slough* is the section named "Damaged." In fact, as we saw in "To a Red Tail," many of DiZazzo's lyrics are songs that risk damages. It's a fallen, imperfect world, from Nixon to Trump, with often more ugliness than grace, whether it's nature's raw chance or the bloody errors of our own blind passions. The characters who are damaged, who populate the poems of "Damaged," do not ask for forgiveness, exculpation, or exemption. They live their fates, and DiZazzo's poems faithfully adhere to the contours of those harmed places. These poems show scars and have reasons to mourn. Still, DiZazzo's lyricism, perfecting the down-line, is ultimately transformational and transcendent. Like the stew cutter's cleaver and the talon of a hawk, DiZazzo's poetic tools are sharp, primal as shards of obsidian glass—an assemblage of honest artifacts that cut true. This transumption in an ordinary hand, throughout, achieves a poetry of real accidentals—here is what takes place, says poem after poem—a blessing and never a complaint.

Consider the movement in these lines from the poem "My Son in a Canoe on the Colorado River": an oar striking the water "pull[s] the river's skin until / it tears / shatters / into / water flies and diamonds," (p. 61). The metaphor of damage turns into a snapshot of Realist and Romantic balance—if DiZazzo's vision is more Diane Arbus than Ansel Adams, he yet reflects the Californian photographer's clarity of sight, a love of the natural world, and a willingness to hone the line until it reflects the visible.

This is not to say that DiZazzo's poems can't be tender or joyous or playful or meditative—they're all that and more. He can be prophetic and mystical, as in the "Coming Attractions" poems (from his early book *Clovin's Head*) and in the otherworldly depictions of mundane visitations transformed into allegory (the poems in the section "Angels"). He can also sound the homespun and downright domestic note, as he takes account of what's close at hand, in poems conveying the wisdom such attention earns (the poem "Edible Abstract," for instance).

Throughout *The Revlon Slough*, DiZazzo's poetic instincts consistently keep paring away at the divisions between the beautiful and the ugly, the Romantic and the Realistic, his words ever edgewise, perfecting that down-line. And when he cuts, he puts neither a bandage nor a bow on it. His poems keep you seeing and feeling. His range is astonishing. From the hiemal chill of "Winter Gulls at Dusk" to the chilly, but in a very different way, "The Suicidals," the poet writes the edges of life, knowing always that these edges become the center, become memory, because here are the details of painful real. I admire the sparseness, the unwillingness to adorn, of these poems that insist on words as tools for seeing, knowing, witnessing.

Ray DiZazzo has written that he learned from many poets in his lifetime of writing, from Sylvia Plath to Rod Mckuen, Pablo Neruda to Charles Bukowski, and he lists Robert Peters and James Dickey as an early influence, whose primal juxtapositions between nature and interloper one might catch here and there in the way DiZazzo directs the startling force of his words. Overall, a reader hears in *The Revlon Slough* a poetic voice coming to terms with the rough and prickly side of language, aptly observing a world where things fall apart. Seldom confessional, DiZazzo writes things as they are, beautiful and damaged. Listening to him make us a bit more whole — because he never forgets it's the cut in the fabric that lets in light. ❧

—Claire Millikin, March 17, 2018
Charlottesville, Virginia

MARVELOUS
CREATURES

TO A **RED TAIL**

Though bound to earth
by size and genus

I have dreamed
your kind of freedom:

belly down, hung
and bouncing on the Santa Anas.

I have scanned the furrows for
a pinkish toe, a flick of ear

a single, sun-caught eye
sparking in the farmland.

And yes, I've felt your gifts:

The

      lift

         and

            roll

                    to

              a perfect

          down-line

    muscled talons
    tightening in fur

    my beak a facial needle
    hooked, inserted, tearing out
    a warm evisceration.

TAILS

For the lynx, a bob
a wooly stub above the anus
shaking off the snow
on a winter slope.

Studs and mares
in southern dust corrals
stand and fly their hairy flags
dropping dung
swatting off the clouds
of gnats and flies.

And dogs?
Thickened whips
tucking under hairless bellies
coiling over, curling sideways
standing, wagging out a figure-eight
of love.

For us nothing
more than a coccyx finger
hook-like, pointing down
in a pelvic X-ray.

But think about
the crocodiles, waving
easily through silt
and lilies

scorpions – the arc-sting
coiled overhead

monkeys
chattering bands
traveling prehensile
through the canopies
of broken shade

and down along
the evolutionary line
"pollywogs" in
reproductive cream
countless tiny trillions
wriggling upstream
in search of eggs.

MICE

Families.
Males, females, pups.

They come in single file
walking tight-rope on the Romex

tiny claws tapping out
the intermittent zaps of TV static.

Here for cheese and retribution
they are fucking in the attics

mounting anything with whiskers
and a breakneck heartbeat

squirting out the pups
in bloody legions.

They've beaten all the traps
left their pellets in the pantry corners

nested in the garden gloves
and rags, peeking out

with eyes as bright
as poppy seeds

and strings of cheddar souring
in teeth the size of porcelain needles.

PIG

I am the boar

meaty giant, prancing
in a blaze of dust and light

my testicles
in tempo slapping

snout upturned, webs of drool
flung from the pinkish folds

of my mouth. Up from the beds
of summer mud, I am strutting

caked, magnificent
among my sows.

THE **WATER** BULLS

The water bulls are wrong.

As round with love
as they may be

as bloated tight
with the tenderness
of weight and dreams

their sun has set for good.

Huddled in the reeds
their crescent horns ringing
with the frequencies of night

they never see, never understand
that stars give off so little
warmth, lunar light is icy

and the calves are
shivering beside them.

SLOTH

*(After paying two dollars to pose
for a picture with an old man
cuddling his pet sloth in Costa Rica.)*

First a paradox:
The yellowed saber claws
and oddly comical snout and face.

Then the eyes:
Almond glass in milk
the slow, crystal blink and gaze
almost comatose with awe
as if she can't believe the saturated hues
sunlit depths and marvelous shapes
her sight has found.

Silver daughter of a distant forest
she is dozing, clutching, dreaming
of a light above the canopies.

KES**TREL**

The secret is to
open, lean

unhook your feet from
creosote and

lift away
from power poles and copper

feeding kitchens
to the south.

The secret is
an altitude of open rings

thermals winding
off the graveled tracks

lifting you in head-locked
focus

to a moment when
the secret is to roll

fall away on a slice of wing
folding

for acceleration
down

a calibrated arc
to something warm

something living
something twitching

in its unsuspecting
whiskers

at the end.

THE VULTURE'S MATH

How slow a movement
is the act of rotting?

How fast the circular descent
from a thousand feet?

How many steps
to walk the side of a zebra's neck

from cheek to shoulder?

BLACK **WIDOW**

1.

I am queen
keeper of the shadowed place.

Threading anything of
permanence to molded earth

I make my rooms.

2.

For you I swell
with a paralytic milk.

I, the polished piece of
shadow, belly-flagged

and hung

among the parts of
motors left too long.

3.

Often in this night
I dream you've come

all my eyes upon your flight
the glittering circles

sunlight into shadow
into silk.

4.
Fangs to gut
we touch and lock.

Your scales are brittle
warm with light.

My face is pulsing
sending in the necessary dose

to stop your muscles
freeze you mind

calm you

for the work
of your cocoon.

5.
I embrace

wind you like a
beating jewel.

A wing, one leg
still moving

pressing out.

My legs are tireless.
They pull, guide, bind.

The gland is like an anus

swelling to release
its thread.

6.
The Moon ascending
light my house

my young
deposited like pearls.

You sleep enclosed
in a gossamer ball

unaware

they have begun at last
to stir.

TOAD **NIGHT** HAIKU

An avocado
sized southern bull, swelling in
the hum of insects

Wı. /ER GULLS AT DUSK

Knowing nothing
of the principles of lift
or why a level sun goes red

one by one

      they open

              rise

      and hang

above the cliffs

held aloft on blusters
off a gray Pacific

January swirls, curling up
the wisps of sand, wailing
through the slatted fences
rolling inland on the waves
of yellow shore grass.

WILDE**BEEST**

It is on TV, the female
down in grass

giving birth

calf's legs, two
like wet black sticks
protruding from the
lump beneath her tail.

Also down
the lioness is closing.

She has calculated this
in terms of energy conserved
hunger, and the appetites
of male and cubs.

I am lounging in the den
drinking beer

feeling, as the kill ensues
at peace.

APPALOOSA

Arc of sunlight
on the spotted rump

skittish, rocking
in a two-horse trailer

stopped (the Chevy honking)
blocking traffic

at the Wynn Street
on-ramp.

THE VULTURES' **GREETING**

Poor Jack

slivered bones in a sandy pelt
opened by an owl at the foot
of an old saguaro.

We are over you in circles.

Can you see us
though your skull-hole full of flies?

We, the feathered pilots
of the canyons and arroyos

               wheeling

        dropping

    hopping

in for lunch

you silly rabbit.

POACHERS

*(Poem for a "No Hunting" sign
in Barstow, California.)*

Though most are satisfied
to flick a cigarette or
sling a bottle

some cannot resist
the paintless metal dents
created by a load of buckshot

Others, liking holes and gashes
use an axe or 30-30.

There are, too, the more "courageous"
who on isolated stretches
take the time

to hang the rabbits
on display.

EVENING **GULLS**

I
      my
            kind

                  are

            falling

         through
   a

   level
         sun

      wheeling

   dropping

turning

      one   by   one   to   silhouettes   along   a   dune.

DAMAGED

CISCO, ME AND
A COPPER ANGEL

Remember me.

Remember
Seventh Street in rain.

Consider
that I found you
crippled in a storm
of jewels

discovered that
the light of opals
sucks the color from
your skin.

Remember
that I bite my nails
remain in shadows.

Keep in mind that
you are virginal
(regardless).

And most of all
remember Cisco
my Italian swan.

He loses feathers
loses weight.
A fever burns
beneath his wings.

Remember
please remember
how he trembled
in your arms.

FARRELL

I am the one
with the chrome-braced leg

walking intersections
half my body
starting up a stairway.

The worst of me (an arm)
is white, freckled
rigid as an insect's.

I am going home
my mother at my side.

You see us through a dirty windshield
crossing.

My head is cocked
my mouth agape, straining

saying, "Father! Father! Father!"
in the speech of frogs.

BEFORE **THE WAKE**

I am waiting in the haze
of your New England parlor
set with doilies and ceramic dogs.

I imagine you are here and say, "Fuck this.
Fuck you all. Get me a gin."

Angelo, of course, pours the Gilbey's
motioning for me to place a Chesterfield
between your lips and flick the Zippo.

Mikey rolls you to the window
where you rap the sill and swear
at two boys passing by the gate.

Dusk light through the blinds
illuminates your woolen blanket
as you draw the smoke in, turn to me
and say again, "Fuck you all."

DWARF

I am walking
toward you

coming

head enlarged
legs bowed out
like a muscled baby.

Taught for this
you look aside
your eyes returning
when I've passed

to see in detail:

pudgy fingers
crooked back
the rump
and full absurdity
of a cowboy's walk.

CELL **18**

Poppy squats
against the bars.

Thumb to a lower lid
he pops a glass eye into his palm.

The socket closes
like a woman's hole.

The eye is milk-glass
with a blue iris.

Poppy rolls it
on the floor

and talks to Jonathan
about his mother.

JUSTICE

Or the one about
the oil king

whose car runs out of gas
in a southern state

who wanders in the forest
for a week

and one night
stumbles senseless

to the door of a backwoods
mad mechanic

who has modified
his truck

to run on
fingernails and piss

and the liquid pressed
from human fat

and needs
to go

to market.

MEMORIES

(For my brother)

My love is in these words
my "fragile" other half
with freckled cheeks
and waterfalls of hair.

And, too, my children
beautiful and brown, bouncing
on their pillows in the den.

You are here with heroin
and magic, cooking dreams
nodding forward into fifteen years
of shame and semi-conscious summers.

Old Moon is in here, too, and both the dogs
and laughing, dancing in our single room
beside the Murphy Bed with Gallo wine
a Kodak Brownie, and their vanishing
New England youths, Mom and Dad
down on Catskill Avenue in Carson.

We are here, all together
leaving one another
very slowly.

WI**NO**

(Huntington Beach '70)

This old
fart

old face
all

sucked in
ripe

old fuzzy
jowled

and drooling
gumming

out his
wrinkled pink

tomato-punctured
mouth

about us
dumb

young

fuckers.

THE **SUICIDALS**

Jesus knew the cross
we know our calibers.

Nails for him
we take the barrels
in our mouths.

We are the saviors
sleeping on the racks of ovens

going breathless
over city bridges
sending out our brains

for sins of yours
on the shower walls.

PORN

It's all about
the
      weight

        and

        dangle

thickness lifting
as the choke-pipe hardens

curling into scissor-locks
and slapping groins.

It's vaginal and swollen
folded to a whiskered smile.

It's rectal, pinched
and all about the lubricant and bruises

heroin, a close-up lens
the yank and squirt of semen

shot across
a butterfly tattoo.

THE **STEW** CUTTER

Over years,
and with the loss of seven fingers

he has learned to swing the cleaver
in the first and third fingers
of his right hand.

His left palm (whitish nubs
and a muscled thumb) is used to situate
and feed the slabs of bleeding meat.

I am waiting for an order
flinching at the blade
as time and time again it sinks

beside the cutter's last thumb.
He glances up and
reading my expression, chuckles.

"Only thing I know," he says
"besides a cleaver and a lean stew
is how to play guitar.

And that's no way
to make a living."

A **FULL PAGE** AD

This in color, captioned
"Give!":

An African boy
with mud-caked legs

stomach, feet and
head enlarged

standing in the sun
a dusty road

his arms (the right extended)
branch-like.

His knees are puffed
leathered apples

a worm-like penis
curling in the space

between his thighs.
He is looking up

staring off the page
at you, as if

about to smile.

THE **LOFT**

The rain has stopped.

There is a moon
and the sweet wet smell of fields.

A spider threads the open beams
its legs like filaments, tapping stars.

This is May. Kimberly
is still alive, and you and I
are making love, our bodies

whiter than the straw.

RE**MEMBER**

*(For Norman,
Huntington Beach, '65)*

Jack-In-The Box
Pacific Coast and Lake.

Sparrows hopping
on the cinder wall.

Traffic backed
boiling in the sun.

Copper girls.

You with the warrant
me on speed

and Jack's giant face
rolling in the sky.

A CRAZY **FUCK**

*(Ferguson, while framing
houses in the summer of '65)*

Six-feet-six
all ligaments and bone
he's a jangling rack
of biker chains and keys.

With soft pack Camels
up-rolled in a T-shirt sleeve
he smiles beneath the dusty bill
of a "Gomez Fill Dirt" ball cap.

He's a crazy fuck
with split-out boots, tremendous
hands, a thirty-two ounce framer's
Vaughan and a shoulder blade
tattoo from the Kama Sutra.

AN **ALCOHOLIC'S** BLESSING

Penguins are
the priests of ice
prisoners the priests
of walls.
I am the priest
of the Jillian's Grill.
Brothers
bless you all!

BI-**PARTISAN** COVERAGE

*"Let's face it. politics is
not for the faint of heart."*
— Chris Mathews, MSNBC

We are on location
lying in the grass, shooting

as the elephant steps
on the side of the Republican's face.

The light is right.
We zoom for a take of the face collapsing

eyeballs slipping from their holes
the one good shriek turning to a kind of

gurgle as the skull and jawbone give
with a set of muffled pops.

Later, after wiping off the lenses
packing tapes and a little snack

it's off to the blue gazebo
for the after-dinner donkey shot

with the Democratic hopeful.

BULLETS

(For Mac)

One

the one you dream about

came between McNeal and you
and found a spot on Captain Wade
above an eyebrow.

      Whistling in

   to a sudden

thump

the muffled bone-crack
sent away a section of his skull
as hard red splatter hit
the sandbags.

He slumped and moaned
a single time   as if thankful
for the chance to sleep.

LOVE SONG FOR A FISHERMAN'S DAUGHTER

She fed me lies
like a meal of sinkers

a shove astern
while the crew was at the bridge.

I sank like steel
off tenth and Spinnaker.

      2:00 A.M.

at The Barracuda Tavern
by the Sea.

24 BY 24

(For Patti, near the end)

So now we have a square

24 by 24.
Everything we need.

Newly carpeted (a desert weave
in sandy Berber) nautical lamps
the quilt with hens your mother made
and of course, the brown recliner.

Three small meals
Pilipino maids and Tuesday Bingo.
Oh, and yes, the en-suite bathroom
with a walk-in shower-tub
and pull string by the toilet.

24 by 24.
~~Everything we need.~~ *A SQUARE*

But up to now
it's been a world unsquared:
a long, chaotic surge of need
and captivation, tenderness and
rage and the soundless calm of

starlit highways winding through
the years of repetitions suns
we thought were endless.

I remember
when the first one founds us
in the little aqua trailer at the beach
and how we learned each other
in that tiny paneled bedroom
shuddering in our children's skins
our backs like chocolate valleys
buttocks smooth and white as milk.

24 by 24.
Everything we need.

GALLERY

MY **SON** IN A CANOE ON THE **COLORADO RIVER**

(For Sean)

Moving out

      from overhang and shadow

         suddenly

           you spark

      human kindling   burning

on the face of a liquid sun.

         Gliding   on the mirrored glaze

   of open water

you dip the oar   pull the river's skin   until

   it tears

      shatters

into

water flies and diamonds

splashing

on a rippled   wide   reflected bend

of Arizona sky.

THE **REVLON** SLOUGH
(For Pete)

"The Calleguas and Conejo Creeks both
penetrate Camarillo farmland, and the
Revolon Slough is located west of the City."
—City of Camarillo, CA
Watershed Report

With no connection to a rouge or lipstick
it has hollowed down to a wound of puddles
overhung with bush, and running jagged
through the Camarillo farmlands.

Strings of silt wave in its shallow pools
dank with the smell of tangled roots
and earth gone bad, home to tunnel webs
families of flies and strutting killdeer.

A single heron stands in the curved shallow
distance, where migrants sit along its banks
in orange afternoons eating boiled pork
and telling tales of spirits in the corn.

HURON

The feel of it

frigid air   afloat on white   hovering

in conifer and pine.

Moccasin crunch
on frost.

Cloud breaths
                curling
        over

shoulder

where he stops

(double feathers
tied in a top-lock)

draws
        holds
                sends

the stone-head arrow

feathers humming
taut as drum skin.

SNIPER

(Vietnam)

At heights like this
horizons bend to haze-arcs
enemy encampments, where
in one today, a tiny general is
stepping from a jungle tent
into the convex gleam of
calibrated glass and cross-hairs.

And far away above this
invisible in face-paint and
a shawl of weeds, you are
lying spread on something like
a precipice in heaven.

Pleased with the lack of wind
tranquil in the solitude of height
and distance, you wrap a finger
on the trigger's iron curve
brace for the stock punch
take the breath
                        exhale

            hold

pull.

DECEMBER 19TH

(For my daughter, at age 3)

You have climbed the couch
in blue pajamas, to the window.

Maple leaves, curled
with the last of Autumn burn

are running on the lawns.
The Pontiac is beaded, cleaned with rain.

Up the block the willows
puff like mating birds.

It is doubtful there is sun, but
I am not at home to say for sure.

SEA STORM

(With my son at Newport, '79)

Turning

on a band of rain
it has come for land

its body

        rolling

   sparking

with the sun-backed
flights

of shore bound
pelicans and gulls.

ON THE **SPEED** OF **SIGHT**

Assume
that being human

we are much too fast
for the sight of plants

that flowers see
at the speed of blooming

grass in movements
of an inch per week

and snails are
even to the fastest roses

scarcely visible shots of light.
Sequoia then, and oak

see the slowest
watching

as the granite slopes
grow like teeth

and constellations
lose their form.

LIGHTNING ON THE **FRONT** NINE

You never see the blue-white fork
caught above you at the apex
of a seven iron backswing.

Two ahead on the seventh Tee
duck reflexively in the rolling crack
then turn to find you standing
in a sand-trap puddle, oddly bent
oddly stiff, smoldering
from your hair and polo.

And in that jolt
that crackling buzz of God
your single shriek bends away
in blinding white magnetic waves   squealing
in the sudden walls of rain
as you tilt, then topple –
a fist-sized hole
sizzling from skull to heel
inside your body.

COPPER

*(On a red-eye flight
above Atlanta)*

Almost gold

and giving light speed
to the flow of voltage

it is fencing off
the continental nights

linking Interstates
and metro-jewels

in necklaces
of filament and neon.

SUMMER **STORMS**

(El Paso, 1967)

Here they rise
and
      swallow.

Sudden dark
       a wind

     first

  drops

popping

 in the dust of porches.

Seconds later
every roof, road

and chicken yard
in steaming rain.

VOYAGER 1

*"Launched in 1977 . . . traveling at over
60 thousand miles per hour, and now,
finally, leaving the rim of our solar system. . .
entering interstellar space."*

—NASA

How far ahead?
How many centuries along the arc
a thing with mass enough
to bend your flight?

Is the night you cross
wormed with howls?
Misshapen mouths?
Light itself
swallowed in the
soundless pools of time?

Is never slowing down

(your catapult across
the interstellar bow shock
to the pull of radiant holes)

a form of answer?

Will you end at something?

Anything?

Or tumble

wingless
calling back

calling back

calling back

across the long forgotten
arc of our existence.

FLOOD

1.

The night the river opens

    Like a long   southern   wound

all breezes

    in the bottom country

die.

Cooling veins

divide   swell   trickle silver

       into valleys

  rising breathless

under gleaming trails   of river stars.

2.

Dawn.

Flowered quilts and couches   sliding easily

    in cold silver.

A terrier   abandoned   leashed

        to its submerged

softening house

floats belly up   inflated   with the cold gas

of swimming circles

                                into shock

3.
Wind rushes from the deep thickets.

Thorned branches   scratch   into the cold

        white silence

                of the dead.

A new sea shivers   breaking clouds

        against deserted white walls.

COMA
(For Sandra)

Seven moons
have risen through this
                    sleep
              this
         dream
    of

         Cadillac and bus

                    colliding
                         soundless

         on a lunar landscape.

Windshields
                    blown

    the glittering clouds

containing   faces

         swollen

              with the pump

of lungs

      of medical

            machines

        of blood

     as thick

as bright

        as liquid silver.

DEATH
(They say it's easy.
Getting there is the bitch.)

Alzheimer's
You might feel odd
uncertain of the date or season
puzzled how those bits of memory
keep turning up half found, half formed
on the tip of your tongue.

Then, one day, it's not alarming
that your neighbor has become your son
your sister, Jean, a principal you knew in school
and Isabel is back from her shallow backyard grave
to screech and flap all night in her attic cage.

Your wife and children watch you go
Thought-by-thought, day-by-day,
until there's nothing left
but neural sputtering and you
alone in a crowded rec. room
oblivious to the smell of bleach and urine
with a vacant stare, more saliva
than your mouth can hold
and no idea who you are.

Stroke

Oxygen! Of course!
The priceless cargo in a pulse of blood.
When deprived, cerebral cells die quickly
but you may not. Maybe just an arm
loosely hinged, swinging from your shoulder
with a white misshapen hand that bounces
off your thigh at every stride. Or possibly
a useless leg, the infamous zombie foot
dragging sideways at the mall.

Seventy years since you've been to school
but now you're listening carefully
mouthing silence, straining
as the rehab coach's lips and tongue
carefully shapes the L's and P's.

A Highway Fatality

Imagine it's a Friday night. You're gliding
almost floating in the comfortable warmth
of an FM jazz tune, seven scotches
and a whispering stream of passing lights.
You drift away in the warble of a solo flute,
miss a curve and send your Honda headlong

off a highway shoulder, bouncing suddenly
through walls of lit-up scrub and frantic bugs.
And for an instant, just a flash in that horrific light
you recognize the trunk of a massive oak.
You know you're gone before the impact.
Or maybe not. Maybe in that final moment
light enfolds you in a crumpling dream
squeezing in the stars and slivers
screeching open, finally, in the Jaws of Life
a sirened journey to a sterile room
where you are lying, staring up
at a team of weary doctors
then moments later staring down
from just above them.

A Holiday Fall
A thoughtless tilt?
A tenth floor balcony above the EL?
One too many Christmas cheers followed
by a joke, a laugh and backward lean
beyond the point where gravity
invalidates the laws of balance.
And all at once you're tumbling
falling wingless through the final moments

of your 29-year life, as the blackened tracks
half packed with snow, leap up
to meet you.

Disease
My mother lived it
just the way Lou Gehrig did.
Thirty-seven months
with the shape of death feeding
in her body.—a spider she could not
regurgitate or shit or piss away or somehow
grab and strangle as it hooked in tight
and drained her organs
shrinking her to sticks
and knots in a leathery hide.
And through it all she kept her mind
smiling often as the spider fed
and her body died around her.

Suicide
Because at first
you'd done it right

the voice is livid.

"Fine" it whispers.
"Valium. A final sleep
acceptable in lieu
of razor blades
a hose and tailpipe
or your husband's .32.

But now remorse?
Suddenly, this need to live?

Well, this my terminal friend
is the Rubicon you've set in motion:

Beginning with your fingertips
and toes, you will crackle inward
joint by joint, to sand.

Your mouth will fill
with roots and you will soon
be wheezing insect wings and ash.

Your shrieks will circle back
in a hurricane of barbs and slivers.

Don't think about the way across
my friend. Don't dream
of the other side
Just sleep."

Old Age

Or, you may go the longest way
bent and shuffling in soiled sweatpants
inching though the Dollar Store behind your walker
coming finally to a time when something simply gives –
perhaps your heart, too tired at a billion beats
to pump once more; your liver, poisoning you finally
after eighty years of beer and scotch without a rest
or the lungs you've burnt and scarred, aching
bubbling up with phlegm and tar.
Or worse, the iridescent fingers
crawling on the ceiling of your skull
inching into fissures, clutching off
your ability to stop the tremors
grasp a spoon or put your right before your left
until you find yourself lying on a bed
strung to the walls with tubes and bags
nurses wandering in and out among the flowers
as you shrink and whiten, drying out like desert linens
staring at the ceiling, pleading
in your mind, for sleep.

AN **END** OF **TIME**

(Time? Some say it is simply
the movement of all things.)

Imagine a thing
we bring to life by
moving through it –
a state incapable of being real
if not in motion.

Picture every galaxy and quasar
every molecule and atom
every Quark, humming String
and hidden Boson seizing up
locking down the infinite arc
of all existence.

Think of starlight bolted still
in a trillion times the density
of stone.

FEBRUARY **HAIKU** FROM A **KITCHEN WINDOW**

Crows in flight, a black
chain at the morning's white throat.
Coffee steams the pane.

WINTER **NOON** **WITHOUT** YOU

(Rockport, Maine, '97)

The boats are out.

There is nothing
on this bay but ice blue sky

rings of pelicans and gulls
deserted moorings.

Winds run out, scratching
at the water's nervous face

in search of sails.

A **PICK-UP** RIDE

(For my wife, son and daughter)

Dripping at the wheel

        splitting fields

    in a leather sweat

      and you out back

          bouncing

     on a hot dirt road

           remnants of hay loads

   wind-shot   swirling off

         a rusted metal bed

    around your faces

laughter

    heads of yellow hair

        gone crazy.

TO**DAY**

(To Sean, with love)

Today
a maple leaf
veined with bolts
of powdery lighting
tumbles off across
the tracks on a warm
Susana wind.

Today
a screen door
squeaks and bangs
its splintered jam
wafting up the dust
beside an open backpack
on a stone house
porch.

Today
a sleeping Mastiff
dreams away the final words
of my existence, turning
everything inside
your heart
to light.

THE **WRECK**

is burning
in the face
behind the
windshield star
at noon at 6th
and Willow
where
the dog
below the
deli window
watching this
collision
pisses at
the screech
and impact
popping out
a balding
forehead
slivers
showering
the tar beside
the Jewish
woman
waiting
at the
light.

THE ASH CLOUD

" . . . a fire burning out of control in Saddleback Canyon . . ."

—News Broadcast

Here in Huntington
it's just the cloud

a soft dirt brown
climbing over those of us
whose fires never leap
the screens

whose heat extremes
are scaled tongues and
thermostats at 80.

Because our shirts
have never smoldered
on our backs

and we have
sprayed our children
only on the summer lawns

because our homes
have never vanished
on the surface of the sun

we hesitate
glance around
continue with the
barbecues and beer

as the day is swallowed
in a soft pale orange
and the kind of rain
this cloud releases
starts to fall.

MIDNIGHT
MOUNTAIN **HAIKU**

A star falls soundless
in the frigid air, sears a
line across the bear.

EGGS

*(For Emily DiZazzo with much
love and some regret.)*

Afternoon.

You are pruning
when the nest is sprung

when (speckled, blue)
three like river stones
fling out.

One ends standing
at the deckchair's foot, leaning
in the circle of its yolk.

Two unbroken in the grass.

Mumbling penance for the first
you rearrange the two surviving
in the cup of twigs and down.

Then you hurry in
to the kitchen window.

You are there at dusk
when the breeze has chilled

when male and female peck
about the nest for a second time

and again fly off.

WESTMINSTER PARK AT EVENING

(With my daughter at age 4)

You tire of the swings
and take to grass

running seagulls
into flight.

I am after you and
closing in.

You bounce and squeal
your hood blown back

the level sun
ablaze in reddish ringlets.

THE **SMELL OF FEATHERS** BOILING

(For my grandmother,
Constanza Simone, with love.)

It was always summer
always in the afternoon.

The knobby feet, straightened
sticking up as if to pinch
from the boiling pot.

And you above me in the steam
busy at the sink
with blood and giblets.

You, who never shuddered
at the smell of feathers boiling

who later
when they'd pull away
so easily, and stick in clumps

to your flattened thumbs
would always sing.

A TRAILER PARK
IN TORNADO ALLEY

Violent storms
are born above these roofs

Cumulus towers
circling in spring

spinning down
the howling fingers

winding through the double-wides
and eight-by-forties

sending up the carts
and poodles

skipping minivans and
carport roofs across the tracks.

SNOW ON **BISHOP FIELDS**
(For S. and M.)

Ghost of ice   it is granular

                                    and

                        floating

                gently

        down

from quiet storms.

Whiteness   leveled out   from where we stand

                        to four horizons

            sending

in its smallest clouds

        our breaths

                words of love

the only warmth for miles

                between our mouths.

IN **THE HIGH** SIERRA

(For Sean)

I found the sky
on a rim of white

a bowl of stones
and glaciers

the face of life held afloat
on clouds so cold

they burned.

DRIVING HOME AT SUNSET

(For Sunday, with love)

Dallas?

Skyline flashes
in a rearview mirror

> *(where you're pushing 40,*
> *with a family, abundant love*
> *and a Boxer dog named Scout).*

El Paso next, then Phoenix
on a straight flat shot to California

> *(as thoughts of you hover*
> *in the heat of passing hills).*

Scrub and yucca landscapes.
Sweltering mounds
inhabited in all directions
by the stands of old saguaros
weathered groups
of single-legged hombres
needled-arms held to the sky
surrendering to the sun

(Of course I love you, yes.
And yes, I'm sorry.
I'm just not sure why.)

as the I-10 points a roasting band
center-lined, humming under Goodyears
shimmering out to a saw-toothed
red horizon.

C O M I N G
ATTRACTIONS

(Four From Clovin's Head)

GIFT — **2032**

Given rightly
in a golden cage

she is one of a pair
of half-mechanical wrens.

Tiny hinges on the feet
a metal beak
the left synthetic wing.

And too
at dawn, when
everything is still

the slightest whirring
as she turns her head
to sing.

BIRTH — **2100**

Face, neck and arms excepted
Loralinn 2 is blue and silver.

She is born with gills
duck-like feet and a taste for minnows.

Taken from the slice in a woman's belly
she is placed at once in a tank with gauges

where she moves about, her tiny mouth
opening and closing.

Loralinn 2, fully grown at 5
and taught (what she needs to know)

will go to work offshore
for the university.

BACK ON THE RANCH — **2118**

This is all inside
beneath a dome.

Near the fences
on a metal pasture
ponies feed.

They are wrapping
pulling tufts of wires
with their tongues.

Many have metallic
parts, riveted jaws
copper hooves
a pewter eye.

The men with
mechanical hands
whose bellies
are a tub of light
are also there

wearing spurs
sitting on the fences
all together
laughing

like a note sustained
by violins.

MOONFIELD — **2127**

Deep in white
the squatting mice

face-to-face
nibbling grain.

Tiny paws
with beaded silver.

Luminous whiskers
twitching.

Eyes like
cameo points

scanning
side to side

back and forth
perpetually

across the star dome.

DREAM **RUBBLE**

TWO DOLLS

The room is empty, bright
and I am with you.

We are seated in a corner.

The floor is wood
whitened with a coat of dust.

Above and to our right
a bare single window glows with sunlight.

Down the wall are
remnants of curtains, shades

wallpaper (stacked blue tulips)
curling at the seams)

a doorless closet, hinges
still intact.

We are leaning,
Side-to-side, head-to-head

like newlyweds in a comedy hit.
It is turning spring.

We have been here
since the day you died.

A **MASSACHUSETTS**
BARN AT **SUNSET**

*(For Uncle Junior, Uncle Frank
and Grandpa)*

You are here   alive again
clomping out in knee-high rubber boots
on fire in the sun, oblivious
to the orange blaze behind you
on the weathered barn-side.

Overalled and laughing
in the smell of radishes and mud
you swing aside the massive doors
lighting up the plow inside, stacks of bushels
rafters sagging under caravans of mice
and corners hung with radiant spiders.

I turn   and when I look again
you've gone, as the valley's shadow
inches up the wall of tools
cooling down the hoes and shovels
graying into dusk, then darkness
on the stairway to the loft.

MARE AND **FOAL**

The mare is lying
on a grass expanse.

Parts of her
against the ground
are cool, damp

wriggling with colonies
of sow bugs.

Ballooned in flies
her belly glistens amber.

The foal (its coat has yet to gleam)
is fuzzy and as if on stilts

beside the mare.

MIDNIGHT EARTH CHANT

Great hard mother   we are
swarming on your back

strapping you in concrete
belts   pumping out your greasy

blood   choking off your blue Pacific
cheeks   as you roll us out beneath

a slice of moon   never dreaming
we are busy with your murder.

EDIBLE **ABSTRACT**

She is lounging in the tub
a sudsy bath.

Her head alone
(a skinned wet cantaloupe) is visible.

Her hair (celery spines in glistening tufts)
is beaded, green, perfect to the curl.

She is winking.

One ewe eye sparkles
with a film of freshness.

Her lipsticked mouth
carved to a luscious smile

is filled (behind the rows
of corn incisors, canines, molars)

with a blood-red
liver tongue.

A **NIGHTMARE** IN THE **DEAD OF WINTER**

I realized
in all my girth and whiteness
I was the snowman
tilted over, top-hat listing
melting at my mother's bedside.

"Mother," I cried,
"The coming sun is the yellow head
of Satan, sending everything we love
slushing off to hell in swollen gutters!

Warmth is the devil's shawl
snow, the sod of heaven
stars, the heads of icy bolts
gleaming in the doors of God!"

She woke with a gasp
shuddering at the size and
blackness of my eyes.

ANGELS

NORTHERN **LIGHTS**

Holy pups

(young Polaris angels
those whose circuits tilt and
whirl the global axis)

sleep in litters   squirming
balls of radiance
and squeals.

And some   in dreams
yawn and stretch   unfolding
yet untested wings

waving up fluorescent curtains
in the northern constellations.

AN**GELS**

Nesting
in the belt of sparks

they chirp in pings
ethereal songbirds

preening wings
and feathered breasts

rising up

     afloat on

          downbeats

   settling back

in the glowing bowls.

A **STARTLED** ANGEL

First the feather-snap
and shriek   and

      for an instant

she is up and

        frozen

           stunned

     her face
a panicked jay

in a moonlit garden.

GUARDIAN ANGELS

I woke and found
they'd come in flocks
and made a place for me

a grove of shadows
sparked with fireflies and pools.

Wings unfolded —
down-swept fans fluttering up

their gowns and halos.
"Here!" they whispered

"Come!" coaxing me across
the rubble of my bones.

EPILOGUE

JUST

(For Patti, with love, Huntington Beach, 1971)

Just a flash
a slice of light

a sword or blade
to carve away
the clouds

plink the stars

and cut you off
a cold white curl
of moon.

Just a glow   a sunrise   orange skies

pinned to the milky ceilings
of your eyes.

Just a breath
a need.

Just you.

ACKNOWLEDGMENTS

Some of these poems have appeared in the following publications

"The Stew Cutter," *Poetry Now*
"Dwarf," *The Berkeley Poetry Review, Poetic Trenches*
"Flood," *Westways*
"Moonfield," *Invisible City*
"Farrell," *Valley Magazine*
"Westminster Park at Evening," *Mother's Manual*
"On the Speed of Sight," *Burning with a Vision* (anthology),
The Alchemy of the Stars (anthology)
"Cisco, Me and a Copper Angel," *California Quarterly*
"The Water Bulls," *SF Poetry Review*
"Two Dolls," *Road Apple Review*
"Cell 18," *Midatlantic Review*
"Back on the Ranch," *The Magazine of Speculative Poetry*
"Guardian Angeles," *The Magazine of Speculative Poetry*
"Moonrunner," *Prelude to Fantasy*
"Justice," *Wilmore City*
"December 19th," *Voices International*
"Voyager 1," *The American Aesthetic*
"Sloth," *Rose Red Review*

"Sniper," *Anthology Americana, Mason J. Press*
"Winter Gulls at Dusk," *Anthology Americana, Mason J. Press*
"The Revlon Slough," *Anthology Americana, Mason J. Press*
"Voyager," *Anthology Americana, Mason J. Press*
"Porn," *Poetic Trenches*
"Tails," *Dime Show Review*

Some of these poems have also appeared in three poetry collections:

Clovin's Head (Red Hill Press, 1976)
Songs for a Summer Fly (Kenmore Press, 1978)
The Water Bulls (Granite-Collen, 2011)

ABOUT **THE POET**

RAY DIZAZZO is an author, filmmaker, and poet. He has appeared on radio and television, taught communication skills to corporate managers in the U.S. and abroad; and has written, produced and directed media and training programs for Fortune 500 clients. DiZazzo has taught intensive producing and directing workshops at the International Film and Television Workshops in Rockport, Maine, California State University, Northridge, and Popular Communications Company in London, England. He delivered a keynote address to employees of the New York State Education Department, and he has spoken to audiences in London, Los Angeles and other U.S. cities. DiZazzo has written a number of communication books, including *The Corporate Media Toolkit: Advanced Techniques for Producers, Writers and Directors* (Focal Press, 2017), *The Clarity Factor: Four Secrets of True Understanding* (Granite-Collen Communications, 2016), which has been translated into six languages, and *Communicate! Confidence Skills for English Learners* (2016). His four-book, Corporate Media Production series has been used in colleges and universities internationally, for over a decade. DiZazzo's has also written several screenplays, one of which was produced and another, currently in development. His work has garnered numerous awards, including the first Los Angeles area Emmy in the Educational category.

DiZazzo's poetry, criticism, essays and fiction have appeared in numerous commercial and literary magazines, newspapers and books, including *The Berkeley Poetry Review, Westways, Mother's Manual, The Easter River Review, Valley Magazine,* and *The Mid-Atlantic Review.* His work has been anthologized in *The Alchemy of Stars, Burning With A Vision,* and *Contemporary Literary Criticism.* In addition, he has published three poetry collections, *The Water Bulls* (Granite-Collen, 2009), *Songs for a Summer Fly* (Kenmore Press, 1978), and *Clovin's Head* (Red Hill Press, 1976).DiZazzo is the recipient of the Percival Roberts Book Award, the Rhysling Award, and is a Pushcart Prize nominee. Having recently retired, he lives in California with his wife of forty-seven years, and spends as much time as possible with his children and grandchildren. ◄

OTHER BOOKS BY
2LEAF PRESS

2LEAF PRESS challenges the status quo by publishing alternative fiction, non-fiction, poetry and bilingual works by activists, academics, poets and authors dedicated to diversity and social justice with scholarship that is accessible to the general public. 2LEAF PRESS produces high quality and beautifully produced hardcover, paperback and ebook formats through our series: *2LP Explorations in Diversity, 2LP University Books, 2LP Classics, 2LP Translations, Nuyorican World Series,* and *2LP Current Affairs, Culture & Politics.* Below is a selection of 2LEAF PRESS' published titles.

2LP EXPLORATIONS IN DIVERSITY

Substance of Fire: Gender and Race in the College Classroom
by Claire Millikin
Foreword by R. Joseph Rodríguez, Afterword by Richard Delgado
Contributed material by Riley Blanks, Blake Calhoun, Rox Trujillo

Black Lives Have Always Mattered
A Collection of Essays, Poems, and Personal Narratives
Edited by Abiodun Oyewole

The Beiging of America:
Personal Narratives about Being Mixed Race in the 21st Century
Edited by Cathy J. Schlund-Vials, Sean Frederick Forbes, Tara Betts
with an Afterword by Heidi Durrow

What Does it Mean to be White in America?
Breaking the White Code of Silence, A Collection of Personal Narratives
Edited by Gabrielle David and Sean Frederick Forbes
Introduction by Debby Irving and Afterword by Tara Betts

2LP UNIVERSITY BOOKS
Designs of Blackness, Mappings in the Literature and Culture of African Americans
A. Robert Lee
20TH ANNIVERSARY EXPANDED EDITION

2LP CLASSICS
Adventures in Black and White
Edited and with a critical introduction by Tara Betts
by Philippa Duke Schuyler

Monsters: Mary Shelley's Frankenstein and Mathilda
by Mary Shelley, edited by Claire Millikin Raymond

2LP TRANSLATIONS
Birds on the Kiswar Tree
by Odi Gonzales, Translated by Lynn Levin
Bilingual: English/Spanish

Incessant Beauty, A Bilingual Anthology
by Ana Rossetti, Edited and Translated by Carmela Ferradáns
Bilingual: English/Spanish

NUYORICAN WORLD SERIES
Our Nuyorican Thing, The Birth of a Self-Made Identity
by Samuel Carrion Diaz, with an Introduction by Urayoán Noel
Bilingual: English/Spanish

Hey Yo! Yo Soy!, 40 Years of Nuyorican Street Poetry,
The Collected Works of Jesús Papoleto Meléndez
Bilingual: English/Spanish

LITERARY NONFICTION
No Vacancy; Homeless Women in Paradise
by Michael Reid

The Beauty of Being, A Collection of Fables, Short Stories & Essays
by Abiodun Oyewole

WHEREABOUTS: Stepping Out of Place,
An Outside in Literary & Travel Magazine Anthology
Edited by Brandi Dawn Henderson

PLAYS
Rivers of Women, The Play
by Shirley Bradley LeFlore, with photographs by Michael J. Bracey

AUTOBIOGRAPHIES/MEMOIRS/BIOGRAPHIES
Trailblazers, Black Women Who Helped Make America Great
American Firsts/American Icons
by Gabrielle David

Mother of Orphans
The True and Curious Story of Irish Alice, A Colored Man's Widow
by Dedria Humphries Barker

Strength of Soul
by Naomi Raquel Enright

Dream of the Water Children:
Memory and Mourning in the Black Pacific
by Fredrick D. Kakinami Cloyd
Foreword by Velina Hasu Houston, Introduction by Gerald Horne
Edited by Karen Chau

The Fourth Moment: Journeys from the Known to the Unknown, A Memoir
by Carole J. Garrison, Introduction by Sarah Willis

POETRY
PAPOLÍTICO, Poems of a Political Persuasion
by Jesús Papoleto Meléndez
with an Introduction by Joel Kovel and DeeDee Halleck

Critics of Mystery Marvel, Collected Poems
by Youssef Alaoui, with an Introduction by Laila Halaby

shrimp
by jason vasser-elong, with an Introduction by Michael Castro
The Revlon Slough, New and Selected Poems
by Ray DiZazzo, with an Introduction by Claire Millikin

Written Eye: Visuals/Verse
by A. Robert Lee

A Country Without Borders: Poems and Stories of Kashmir
by Lalita Pandit Hogan, with an Introduction by Frederick Luis Aldama

Branches of the Tree of Life
The Collected Poems of Abiodun Oyewole 1969-2013
by Abiodun Oyewole, edited by Gabrielle David
with an Introduction by Betty J. Dopson

2Leaf Press is an imprint owned and operated by the Intercultural Alliance
of Artists & Scholars, Inc. (IAAS), a NY-based nonprofit organization that
publishes and promotes multicultural literature.

NEW YORK
www.2leafpress.org